MONSTER MYSTERIES

Many people claim to have seen mysterious
monsters, such as the yeti, the Loch Ness monster
and other lesser-known creatures. Reports have
been made and scientists have tried to disprove the
sightings, calling them mirages or cases of mistaken
identity. A great deal of research has been carried
out to try to prove the existence of these animals,
from early photographic documentation to
advanced scientific probing, which has,
unfortunately, so far been unsuccessful. As you
read through this book, try to decide for yourself
whether or not these strange monsters exist.

As Scotsman Arthur Grant made his way home in 1934, he saw the Loch Ness monster in the middle of the road. Swerving, he narrowly missed a collision . . .

MONSTER MYSTERIES

Rupert Matthews

Illustrated by Bernard Long

The Bookwright Press
New York · 1989

Great Mysteries

Ancient Mysteries
Lands of Legend
Lost Treasures
Monster Mysteries
Sea Mysteries
UFOs

Cover illustration: A yeti struggles through a snowstorm on the slopes of the Himalayas.

First published in the
United States in 1989 by
The Bookwright Press
387 Park Avenue South
New York, NY 10016

First published in 1988 by
Wayland (Publishers) Limited
61 Western Road, Hove
East Sussex BN3 1JD, England

Library of Congress Cataloging-in-Publication Data

Matthews, Rupert
   Monster mysteries.

   (Great mysteries)
   Summary: Discusses sightings, available evidence, and other information
on such elusive monsters as the yeti, Congo dinosaur, and Loch Ness monster.
      1. Monsters — Juvenile literature. [1. Monsters]
I. Title   II. Series: Great mysteries (Bookwright Press)
GR825.M23   1988   001.9'44   87-31479
ISBN 0-531-18218-5

Phototypeset by Oliver Dawkins Ltd., Burgess Hill, West Sussex RH15 9LH.
Printed in Italy by G. Canale & C.S.p.A., Turin.

Contents

Introduction

Sometimes newspapers or magazines carry strange stories about mysterious monsters, such as the sasquatch or the sea serpent. These reports often take the form of an eyewitness account by a person who claims to have seen some strange and unknown animal. Often the newspaper has asked a scientist for a statement. Usually the scientist will say that a creature such as that reported does not exist. He or she may suggest that the witness saw a mirage or perhaps a strangely shaped tree trunk.

Most people have read reports of this kind. Usually the sighting of a strange animal is soon forgotten. But are the scientists correct when they say that large animals unknown to science do not exist? Many people think not.

As more and more people report seeing strange animals, the evidence builds up. Many of those who claim to have seen such animals are highly respected. It is unlikely that they are inventing the story. The strange animals are often said to be seen at very close range and in considerable detail. It is therefore difficult for the witnesses to be mistaken in what they see.

Coniferous forest under snow, Mount St. Helens region in the state of Washington. These are the sorts of conditions in which the sasquatch would have to survive during the long winter months.

These mysterious monsters take a variety of forms. This book reviews the evidence offered to support the existence of animals such as the Loch Ness monster, the yeti and the sucuriju. It might seem that there is enough evidence to prove the reality of these creatures. However, scientists impose strict rules on such evidence. To confirm the existence of a species of animal, an individual specimen must be available for study.

None of the animals in this book has yet been proved to exist. When you have finished reading the evidence contained here, perhaps you can decide for yourself whether the animals really exist or whether they do not . . .

Above *This "ape-man" was found very near the Venezuela/Colombia border by Francois de Loys in 1929. It is now thought to have been a type of spider monkey.*

Left *A famous photograph of the Loch Ness monster, taken on April 19, 1954 by a London surgeon, R. K. Wilson.*

7

A fishing trip disturbed

Loch Ness, a lake in Scotland, is calm and still. On this July evening in 1963, Mr. MacIntyre and Mr. Campbell are fishing for trout in the loch. The boat rocks slightly as if another boat has passed by, but no other craft is in sight.

Suddenly something disturbs the water close to the fishermen. They look at the spray and waves in surprise. Their surprise turns to shock and fear when a huge neck and head rear up from the water. Water cascades down from the head as it thrusts up into the air. The fishermen are stunned. They stare at the monstrous sight in front of them. The monster seems to look at the fishermen and their boat. Then it sinks back beneath the water. The monster does not dive. It seems simply to sink vertically.

A few seconds later the head and neck appear again, but farther away. The monster disappears once more. The fishermen stare at the waters of the loch for a time. Then they hurriedly row back to the shore and scramble onto land. Asked about his encounter some time later, Mr. MacIntyre says: "There is certainly a weird beastie in the loch."

The Loch Ness monster

For hundreds of years Loch Ness was a strange and remote place. Enclosed by steep mountains, the dark waters of the loch were visited only by locals and a few visitors. Even then there were stories of a strange animal swimming in the waters. But few outsiders visited the huge body of water, and the tales were not taken seriously. However, everything changed in 1933.

In that year a wide, modern road was built along the northern shore of Loch Ness. The road runs beside the loch for all of its 35-km (22-mi) length and offers good views over the dark waters. Thousands of people began to travel on this road. On May 2, 1933, one of these people told a strange story to a local newspaper.

John Mackay, who lived in Inverness, said that he had been driving beside the loch when he noticed something in the water. The surface of the loch was calm and still, but at one place there was a lot of spray and churning water.

The Loch Ness monster as it might look in its natural habitat.

Trapped in the loch?

1. One theory states that the monsters became trapped in the loch. About 10,000 years ago, the last ice age ended. Sea water covered that area that is now Loch Ness. Sea monsters lived in those waters, possibly because they would have been fairly calm and sheltered.

2. Over the years, the land rose up, cutting off Loch Ness and the monsters from the sea. The Loch changed slowly from salt to fresh water. The monsters adapted to the fresh water conditions and survived by living off the fish in the lake.

Mackay stopped to watch. He saw a huge object, which looked like the back of a whale, rise up above the surface of the loch. The object was in sight for about a minute before it sank out of view. In the report the newspaper called the animal a "monster."

Over the following months many people reported seeing the monster in Loch Ness. A few people snapped blurred photographs of the object. Most people saw only a large shape moving in the water, but some were more lucky. They said they had seen a long neck and small head. In April 1934, one man even photographed the neck and head. This picture, taken by Mr. R. K. Wilson, shows a neck rising from the loch, with a small head on top. A large body can be seen below the surface.

The picture caused great excitement. Scientists, however, were not impressed. They pointed out that most people had seen the monster at a distance. They could not give any details of the animal's appearance. Perhaps they had really seen something quite ordinary that only appeared to be a monster. The photographs were said to be either fakes or pictures of ordinary objects. Scientific disbelief and the start of the World War II meant that for some time interest in the monster slackened.

According to Robert H. Rines, this photograph shows the fin of the Loch Ness monster. This and other pictures, taken by Rines in 1972, were backed up by sonar contacts with a large creature.

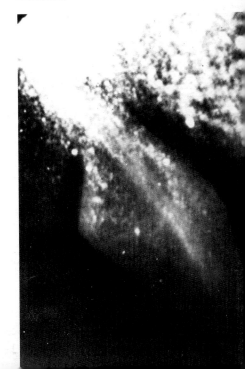

The depths of the loch

Loch Ness is one of the deepest lakes in Britain. It reaches a maximum of at least 225 m (740 ft), though some claim that it is even deeper. Very little of this vast depth is actually inhabited. The vast majority of fish live in the 30 m (100 ft) of water closest to the surface. If the monster exists, it would therefore have to come to the surface waters to find its food.

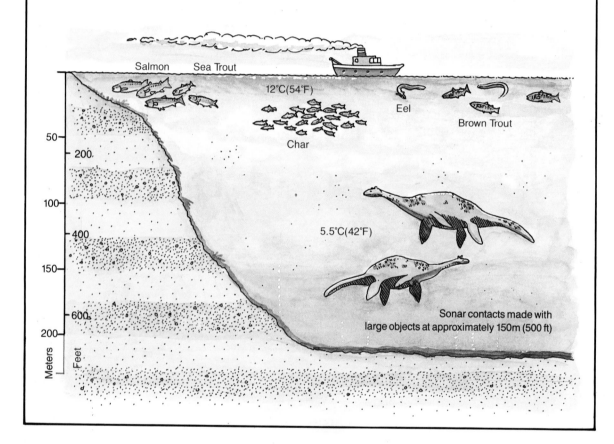

In the 1960s people became interested in the monster once again. On April 23, 1960, a visitor to the area named Tim Dinsdale had a movie camera with him when he saw the monster. Dinsdale shot four minutes of film of a large object moving across the loch. Unfortunately the object was too far away to be seen in detail. Photographic experts said that the film showed a genuine object moving through the water. But scientists still remained skeptical.

According to scientific principle, no animal can be considered to exist until scientists have a specimen to study. A photograph alone will not convince scientific authorities that a previously unknown animal exists.

In 1969 a boat was sent out onto Loch Ness with a sonar

device. Sonar sends out pulses of sound and measures any echoes that come back. By analyzing these echoes, the equipment can detect any objects under the water. The sonar picked up a large object moving at a depth of about 150 m (500 ft). Other sonar equipment detected large objects moving far beneath the surface. It seemed that there was something large in Loch Ness, but was it a monster?

In 1972 the Massachusetts Institute of Technology sent a team of scientists to the loch. They set up a sonar combined with a camera. The equipment was designed so that if anything swam close to the sonar, the camera would photograph it. Three impressive photographs were taken that seemed to show a large animal. Unfortunately the murky water made the pictures indistinct and blurred.

While all this activity was taking place under the water, the monster was seen on the surface by many people. From all these sightings it was possible to build up a picture of the Loch Ness monster. Most descriptions agree that the animal

In August 1960, the Lowrie family were cruising in their boat when they spotted a strange object following them. As it came closer, they could make out a body and a neck. Frightened, they altered course to avoid the monster, and soon lost sight of it.

FINOLA

has a large body, which usually remains beneath the water. A long neck carries a small head, which often pokes up above the water. The creature probably swims by means of four powerful flippers. One of the underwater photographs appeared to show a flipper. The monster seemed between 6 and 9 m (20-30 ft) long. In 1972 two scientists studied the number of fish in Loch Ness. They decided that there were indeed enough fish in the loch to feed a population of large animals, like the monster.

In October 1987, Operation Deepscan, led by Adrian Shine, swept the waters of Loch Ness with sonar equipment. While the project reported contact with several large objects, it was not proved that any of these were the elusive monster.

Urquhart Castle, on the shore of Loch Ness, has been the scene of several mysterious "Nessie" sightings.

Date chart

c.565 St. Columba visits Loch Ness and frightens away "a very odd looking beastie" by his holy power.

1933 The building of a new main road opens Loch Ness to many outside visitors.

1933-1939 Many sightings are reported and several photographs are taken.

1969 Sonar equipment shows several large objects moving in Loch Ness.

1972 An underwater camera takes three pictures of what seems to be a monster.

1987 Organized watch continues to be kept at Loch Ness by many enthusiasts.

Despite the efforts of many dedicated people, no conclusive proof has yet been found to prove that there is a monster in the loch. Every summer teams of volunteers keep a close watch on Loch Ness. They are armed with cameras and other instruments. Perhaps they will one day gather convincing evidence that a monster exists.

It is interesting that Loch Ness is not the only lake that is supposed to have a monster. A similar large creature has been reported in nearby Loch Morar. Farther away, in Ireland, several lakes are said to have strange animals living in them. Most of these lakes are in County Mayo and County Kerry in the west, where the landscape is similar to that around Loch Ness.

Thousands of miles away in North America, other lake monsters have been seen. Lake Okanagan, in British Columbia, has been reported as the home of an animal that looks like an enormously long water snake. It seems that large lakes house far more than fish!

Operation Deepscan, October 1987, a fleet of boats carrying sonar equipment begin their search for the monster.

A photograph of "Nessie," taken by Anthony Shiels in 1977.

The *Daedalus* incident

It is late in the afternoon of August 6, 1848. H.M.S. *Daedalus* is in the South Atlantic, sailing home after four years at sea. The weather is overcast and dull. The events about to take place are to be anything but dull.

Midshipman Sartoris is gazing idly out to sea. He sees something moving in the sea. He looks more carefully and cries out in surprise. Lieutenant Drummond comes over to see what is the matter. Sartoris points out the approaching object. Drummond calls Captain M'Quhae over. Together with the master and three sailors, the officers watch an amazing sight . . .

Approaching them is a truly enormous sea serpent. The creature is at least 18 m (60 ft) long. It holds its head and neck out of the water and swims steadily past the ship. The monster passes close enough for the men to see every detail, but it does not seem to notice the ship. As the mysterious animal passes out of sight, the officers watch it through a telescope. By the time it disappears, the sea monster has been in sight for 20 minutes.

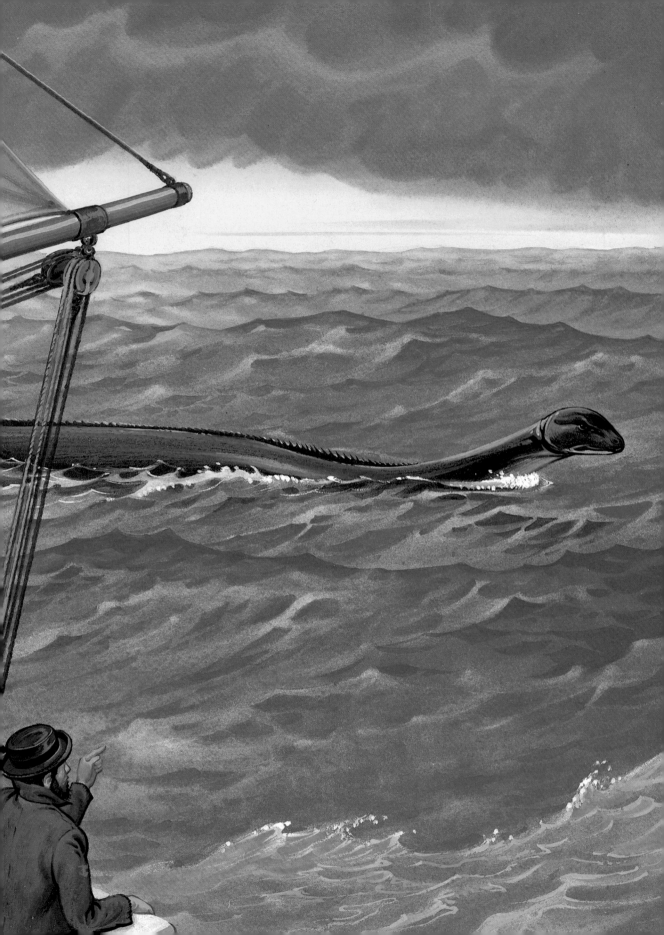

Sea monsters

For centuries sailors have been telling stories about huge animals living in the seas. Many of these stories were simply invented to impress the people who stayed on land. However, several reports of large sea creatures were made by responsible people who were prepared to swear that their stories were true.

The case of Captain M'Quhae is a typical example. As a captain in the Royal Navy, M'Quhae was experienced enough to recognize nearly every large sea animal in existence. Even though the creature passed so close to the ship that M'Quhae could give a detailed description, he still could not say what type of animal it was. An equally dramatic event occurred on June 2, 1877. The British Royal Yacht *Osborne* was cruising through the Mediterranean and had just passed Sicily when three officers saw a very large animal, at least 16 m (52 ft) long. It surfaced close to the ship and quickly swam away. The creature had a large, wide body with two enormous flippers. In front of the body was a long neck and a small head. No one could say what it was.

In 1962 the Frenchman Robert Le Serrec was sailing

A sea monster seen off Greenland by Hans Egede in 1734.

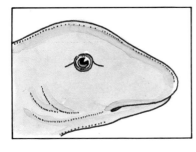

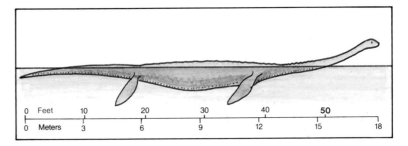

0	Feet	10	20	30	40	50	
0	Meters	3	6	9	12	15	18

along the Great Barrier Reef, off the Australian coast. He spotted a large dark animal resting in the shallow water of the reef. The creature looked like a huge serpent, about 20 m (65 ft) long. When Le Serrec tried to swim up to the monster, it dived into deeper water.

Le Serrec's report is unusual because it is fairly modern. Most sightings took place many years ago. This does not mean that sea serpents are now extinct, nor that old-time sailors were more likely to invent stories. The noise of modern ship engines may well frighten sea animals away. It is also true that large modern ships need fewer men as crew than the old sailing ships. This means that there are fewer people on the high seas with the chance to see these creatures. It is, therefore, not surprising that only a few reports of sea serpents have been made in recent years.

Above Drawings of the Daedalus sea serpent, based on observations made at the time of the sighting.

Date chart

1734 The first reliable report of a sea serpent is made by Hans Egede, who saw a monster off the coast of Greenland.

1848 A large unknown animal is seen by the crew of H.M.S. *Daedalus.*

1877 A huge creature with flippers and a long neck is seen by officers of the British Royal Yacht *Osborne.*

1962 Robert Le Serrec spots a serpent-like animal in the sea off Australia.

"Morgawr," the British sea monster, photographed during February 1976 from Rosemullion Head, near Falmouth, Cornwall.

19

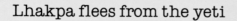

Lhakpa flees from the yeti

Lhakpa Sherpani sits down on the grass to relax. All through this summer morning in 1975 she has been hard at work. Lhakpa has had to drive her yak herd up from the valley to this high pasture land. Now the yaks are grazing peacefully and Lhakpa can rest for a short while.

Suddenly, Lhakpa is alert again. She can hear something large moving in the undergrowth. Lhakpa peers into the bushes in concern. Perhaps the noise is being caused by a bear or tiger. Suddenly, the creature bursts into the open. Lhakpa gasps in alarm. She can hardly believe what she is seeing. In front of her stands a yeti!

While Lhakpa watches in horror, the yeti looks around at the girl and her yaks. The yeti opens its mouth and lets out a loud, piercing howl. The strange creature then runs forward. Lhakpa screams and runs back down the hill toward her village. The yeti ignores her, but chases after the yaks. It seems to be after one small calf. As Lhakpa flees she turns to see the yeti chasing the calf and the yaks stampeding around the pasture.

Yeti: the "man-thing"

About 150 years ago British soldiers, civil servants and big-game hunters began to travel in the Himalayas. They heard some very strange stories indeed. The local people, including Sherpas, told the British that fierce hairy men lived in the mountains. Though several British visitors recorded the tales, they did not believe them.

Then, in 1889, Major Waddell saw strange tracks in the snow of the Himalayas. He asked some Sherpas what animal had made the tracks. The Sherpas assured him that a yeti, or "man-thing" was responsible. Over the following years many travelers came across strange footprints. News of these footprints spread, and soon the yeti became the subject of scientific debate. Some scientists thought that the yeti could exist, while others dismissed it as a figment of the imagination. In 1951 startling new evidence emerged.

Two mountaineers, Eric Shipton and Michael Ward, were climbing on the Menlung Glacier at a height of 6,000 m

A sherpa examines footprints in the snow and declares that they were made by a yeti (Daily Mail Himalayan Expedition, 1954).

(20,000 ft). Shipton and Ward were startled to see a line of footprints. The tracks were not human, but they were fresh. Unlike others who had seen supposed yeti tracks, Shipton had a camera. He chose the clearest footprint and took a photograph of it.

The picture showed a footprint that was unlike that of any known animal. Nobody has been able to explain what type of animal made the print, and it remains the most important piece of evidence for the existence of the yeti.

It is from mountaineers that the most important modern evidence for the existence of the yeti has come. In 1975, Janusz Tomaszczuk, a Pole, came face to face with what he claimed to be a yeti. He described the beast as being similar to an ape over 2 m (6½ ft) tall. In 1979 an expedition mounted by the British Royal Air Force brought back more pictures of footprints. Some mountaineers, such as Chris Bonnington of England, have even started to place yeti-hunting among the aims of their expeditions.

Above The southwest face of Mount Everest. It is on the snow-covered slopes of the Himalayas that many yeti tracks have been found.

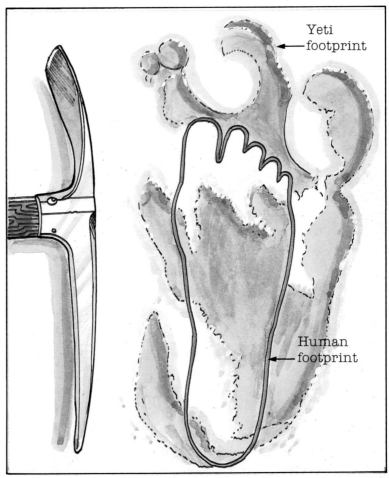

Yeti footprint

Human footprint

Right A yeti footprint found by Eric Shipton in 1951, with a human footprint superimposed.

Because reports by mountaineers and Western visitors are so scanty, researchers interested in the yeti have turned to the Sherpas for information. The Sherpas seem to regard the yeti as a perfectly normal animal, in the same way as they think of bears or monkeys. However, Sherpas often seem to be frightened when they think that a yeti is nearby.

According to the stories told by the Sherpas, there are two types of yetis. First there is the dzu-ti. This is a large animal, standing nearly 3 m (10 ft) tall, which is aggressive and dangerous. It seems to have been a dzu-ti that attacked the yaks being herded by Lhakpa Sherpani. A smaller type of yeti is the meh-ti. This harmless creature usually runs off when it meets a human.

Both types of yetis are said to live in the dense forests just below the snowline, though they often roam the high peaks. It is among the peaks that the high-pitched whistling call of the yeti is most often heard. Yetis are described as being covered with hair, which is longer on their heads than on their bodies, though their faces are generally bare. The yetis are said to move most often on all fours. They will bound along using their hind feet and the knuckles of their front limbs. From this description it seems that the yeti is a type of large ape. It is possible that it resembles a gorilla or an orangutan. From fossil evidence it is known that apes lived in this mountain area only a few thousand years ago. Perhaps the yeti is an isolated descendant from earlier times.

24

Date chart

1832 The first mention of a yeti by a European. B. H. Hodgson records native tales in Nepal.

1889 Major Waddell comes across strange footprints in Sikkim.

1951 Eric Shipton takes his famous photograph of a yeti footprint in Tibet.

1975 Janusz Tomaszczuk meets a yeti near Mount Everest.

1988 European mountaineers remain on the alert in case they find yeti footprints or even yetis themselves.

Opposite In June 1970, Don Whillans was camping on the snowfields in a shallow valley in the Himalayas. Hearing noises outside his tent, he looked out to see a yeti scurrying toward the trees on all fours.

Below left and right This hand and scalp, owned by monks at Pangboche Monastery in Nepal, are supposed to be those of a yeti. Skeptics have claimed that the hand is really a human hand and that the "scalp" was molded out of goat skins.

This theory is not too farfetched. There are plenty of densely forested valleys in the Himalayas where a group of large apes could have found enough food to survive.

The Himalayas are not the only place in Asia where strange stories of hairy ape people are told. Throughout northern China, Mongolia and eastern Russia the local people report encounters with creatures called almas. Unlike the yetis, the almas are not looked upon as animals by local residents. They believe that the almas are real, but very primitive and inferior, people.

It is interesting that the description given by Asians of almas and their culture is very similar to the picture of Neanderthal people built up from archaeological finds. The Neanderthal people were a separate sub-species of humans who died out about 40,000 years ago. Some scientists think that isolated tribes of Neanderthals may still survive in the remote areas of Asia. However, there is little evidence, other than the stories of local people, to support this idea.

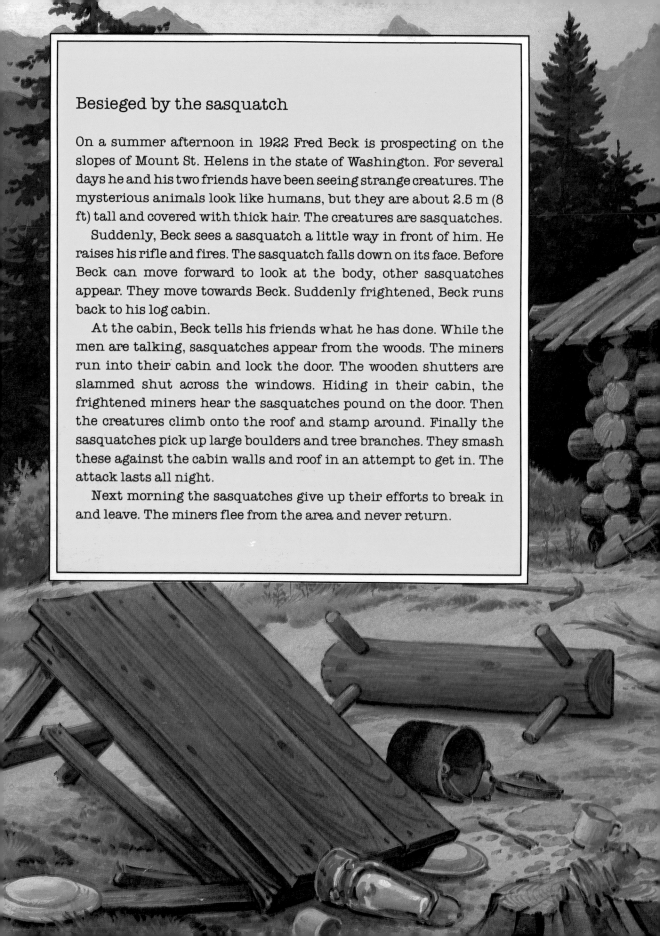

Besieged by the sasquatch

On a summer afternoon in 1922 Fred Beck is prospecting on the slopes of Mount St. Helens in the state of Washington. For several days he and his two friends have been seeing strange creatures. The mysterious animals look like humans, but they are about 2.5 m (8 ft) tall and covered with thick hair. The creatures are sasquatches.

Suddenly, Beck sees a sasquatch a little way in front of him. He raises his rifle and fires. The sasquatch falls down on its face. Before Beck can move forward to look at the body, other sasquatches appear. They move towards Beck. Suddenly frightened, Beck runs back to his log cabin.

At the cabin, Beck tells his friends what he has done. While the men are talking, sasquatches appear from the woods. The miners run into their cabin and lock the door. The wooden shutters are slammed shut across the windows. Hiding in their cabin, the frightened miners hear the sasquatches pound on the door. Then the creatures climb onto the roof and stamp around. Finally the sasquatches pick up large boulders and tree branches. They smash these against the cabin walls and roof in an attempt to get in. The attack lasts all night.

Next morning the sasquatches give up their efforts to break in and leave. The miners flee from the area and never return.

The sasquatch

Opposite *A statue of a sasquatch at Willow Creek, California.*

Mrs. Chapman, of Ruby Creeks, Washington, had just finished baking an apple pie and was putting it on the window sill to cool, when she saw a huge sasquatch walking toward her house! Terrified, she ran screaming from the house, and did not stop for nearly a mile. Presumably, the sasquatch has been attracted by the smell of the pie.

The far western area of the North American continent is a wide and untamed wilderness. Vast forests cover steep mountains and hidden valleys. This huge, trackless area of forest and mountain covers the states of Oregon, Washington and parts of California and Idaho, together with large parts of the Canadian provinces of British Columbia and Alberta. It is here that the mysterious creature called the sasquatch is said to live.

The first recorded mention of the sasquatch was by David Thompson. He was exploring the mountains of Alberta in 1811 when he found some strange tracks. Thompson's guide told him that they had been made by the sasquatch, a huge hairy person. Thompson did not believe the guide. Over the following years several trappers and explorers repeated tales of the sasquatch. It was the dramatic and frightening experience of Fred Beck and other events that made the sasquatch famous.

Over the past 40 years interest in the sasquatch has increased steadily. Many people have traveled through the forests looking for evidence that the sasquatch exists. Thousands of sasquatch footprint tracks have been found,

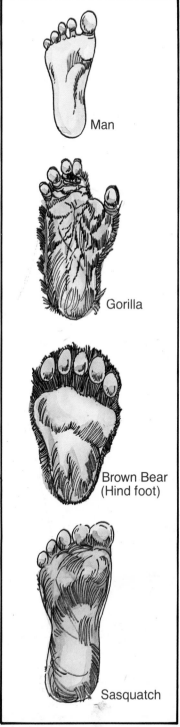

Below How human footprints compare with those of the sasquatch and other animals.

Man

Gorilla

Brown Bear
(Hind foot)

Sasquatch

photographed and copied in plaster. It is the sheer size of these prints that has given the sasquatch the name by which it is known in the United States. It is called Bigfoot!

Scientists have studied the footprints in great detail. Some have decided that the tracks are fakes. They might have been produced by a person wearing shoes with big wooden feet strapped to them, or by a simple stamp on a stick. Other scientists are not so sure.

Footprints can be used to create a picture of the type of animal that produced them. The sasquatch prints vary in size, averaging about 40 cm (16 in) long by 16 cm (6 in) wide. The footprint is slightly different from that of a human, being shaped like an hour-glass rather than having one straight side and one curved. Judging by these footprints the sasquatch is able to walk on two legs, is about 2.5 m (8 ft) tall and weighs more than 150 kg (330 lb).

This is exactly the creature described by the eyewitness accounts of dozens of people who claim to have seen the mysterious creature. In 1955 Bill Roe, a trapper in Alberta, Canada, was pushing through some bushes when he spotted a sasquatch only about 6 m (20 ft) away. As Roe watched, the animal ate some leaves before moving off.

Above *Trapper Bill Roe's encounter with a sasquatch in Canada in 1955.*

Left *A frame from a movie film of a sasquatch taken by Roger Patterson on October 20, 1967, at Bluff Creek, California.*

Opposite *This map shows the places where evidence of ape-like people have been found.*

Bill Roe's sighting is one of the few to indicate the lifestyle of the sasquatch. Other reports speak of the sasquatch eating small animals. This raises the interesting question of whether or not the sasquatch could actually feed itself in the western forests.

The sasquatch, if it exists, is a large animal, so it would need a large amount of food to survive. The coniferous forests in which the sasquatch is sighted are not rich in food. During the summer months there is probably enough food to keep a large number of these creatures alive and healthy. However, in the winter the food supply drops off as snow covers the land. If the sasquatch exists, it would either need to leave the forests or hibernate. The only way in which the sasquatch could survive in the cold weather would be to store up food during the summer. It would then be possible for it to live off these food supplies during the cold months of winter.

The evidence for the existence of the sasquatch is strong. There are many eyewitness sightings and plenty of footprints for scientists to study. It is just possible that such an animal could survive in the forests, but there is no conclusive proof that it does. Despite the sightings and footprints, nobody has ever shot or captured a sasquatch and shown it to scientists. Until this happens, the animal will remain on the fringes of science.

Date chart

1811   David Thompson sees strange footprints and is told about the sasquatch.

1922   Fred Beck and his party are attacked by sasquatches.

1955   Bill Roe sees a sasquatch at short range.

1960s   Dedicated sasquatch hunters roam in the backwoods to look for traces of the sasquatch.

1980   Accumulated evidence is subjected to scientific research, but still no conclusive proof of the existence of the sasquatch is found.

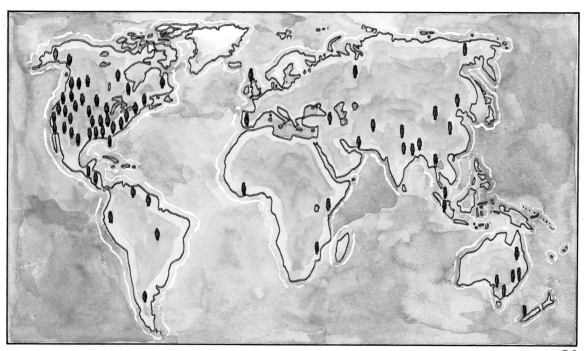

The battle in the swamp

It is a warm morning in the swamps bordering Lake Bangeweulu in modern-day Zambia. Three canoes are paddled cautiously by a party of hunters. Armed with sharp spears, the men in the canoes are looking for hippopotamuses to kill for food. Crocodiles are found in these waters as well as hippopotamuses. The hunters know they must be careful.

Suddenly, a huge animal splashes into view from among some reeds. It glares fiercely at the canoes. One of the older men recognizes the animal. He shouts out "chipekwe!" and steers his canoe toward the beast. As soon as they are close enough, the men throw their spears at the large animal. Several hit it.

The chipekwe roars in pain and lashes out with its tail. It turns toward the canoes and attacks them with its legs and tail. The canoes and the men retreat before the beast.

Then they return to the attack. This time one of the canoes is overturned by the chipekwe and the men are thrown into the water. The fight rages for several hours. Eventually, the beast weakens from the many spear wounds it has suffered. The chipekwe collapses into the water and the hunters return home in triumph.

The African dinosaur

Africa is a vast continent. It covers millions of square miles. Despite the fact that modern maps show mountain ranges and rivers, there are parts of Africa that are still relatively unexplored.

Today it is far easier to fly between towns than to drive along rough, uncomfortable roads. This means that air transportation has become common, while many roads and tracks have fallen out of use. At the heart of the continent are the massive swamps of the Congo basin. Few people live in these swamps, which spread over thousands of square miles. Only around the edge of the basin is there a scattering of villages.

It was from these villages and swamps that news came that was to amaze scientists. In 1919 Mr. C. E. James went home to Britain after spending eighteen years in the area around

In 1920, a hunter named Lepage spotted a large animal near a swampy river and took a shot at it. He missed, and the creature chased him for some distance. He had encountered the mokele-mbembe!

Lake Bangeweulu. He told a remarkable story about an animal that the local tribesmen called a chipekwe. The chipekwe is known in many other places as the mokele-mbembe.

James based his description of the chipekwe, or mokele-mbembe, on the evidence of tribesmen. They told him that the animal was bigger than a hippopotamus, had a barrel-shaped body and a long neck and tail. On the tip of its snout, the mokele-mbembe was said to have a small ivory horn. The description of the mokele-mbembe was very similar to that of sauropod dinosaur fossils that had been found. This led several people to believe that the mokele-mbembe was a dinosaur.

The sauropod dinosaurs, such as *Diplodocus*, were a group of reptiles that lived throughout the world between 195 and 65 million years ago. The sauropods are believed to have died out along with all the other dinosaurs about 65 million years ago, and there is no evidence that any dinosaurs survived. However, no one can be sure that some did not. Whatever the truth of the matter, a very large animal of

__Above__ Sauropod dinosaurs lived on earth between 195 and 65 million years ago.

__Below__ A weight used by local traders in the Congo basin region, made in the shape of a mokele-mbembe.

unknown type is reported to be living in the heart of Africa. There are many other reports from different areas of the same type of animal living in swampland. The pygmies, for instance, tell stories of an animal 16 m (52 ft) in length, with a long neck and tail. The people concerned are nearly always cut off from each other geographically, so it is unlikely that they could exchange stories. It would seem that the only explanation for these similar reports is that such an animal actually exists.

The mokele-mbembe is the best reported of all these creatures. For several years King Lewanika of the Barotse

Above Dinosaur hunter Herman Regusters points to the Congo, as he describes sightings of a creature the size of two hippos in Lake Tele.

Right In 1932, explorers were surprised by a mokele-mbembe as they paddled down a river in the Cameroons.

36

tribe passed on to scientists all the reported sightings of the mokele-mbembe brought to him by his subjects. On one occasion, the King himself saw the trail of the elusive creature.

In 1919 Captain Leicester Stevens, an Englishman, set out to hunt the "Congo Dinosaur," as he called it. Due to poor planning, Stevens never even reached the Congo! Slightly more successful was the American James Powell who visited the Congo in the 1970s. He talked to local tribesmen and recorded their stories. He showed the Congolese people pictures of various animals. When he held out a picture of a sauropod dinosaur, the local people identified it as a mokele-mbembe. However, nothing could be proved by this. It still remains unlikely that a dinosaur has survived for millions of years. But if these eyewitnesses are not seeing a dinosaur, nobody has yet explained what they *are* seeing. Surely these Congolese people are not imagining things?

Ambitious plans are being prepared by Professor Roy Mackal of the University of Chicago. He has already visited the Congo swamps and now plans to return in an attempt to capture a mokele-mbembe. Mackal is convinced that there is some kind of large animal living in the remote swamps. There are not many scientists who would agree with him. However, if the dinosaur hunt were to be successful, there are many Africans who would not be at all surprised — after all, they have been telling people about them for years.

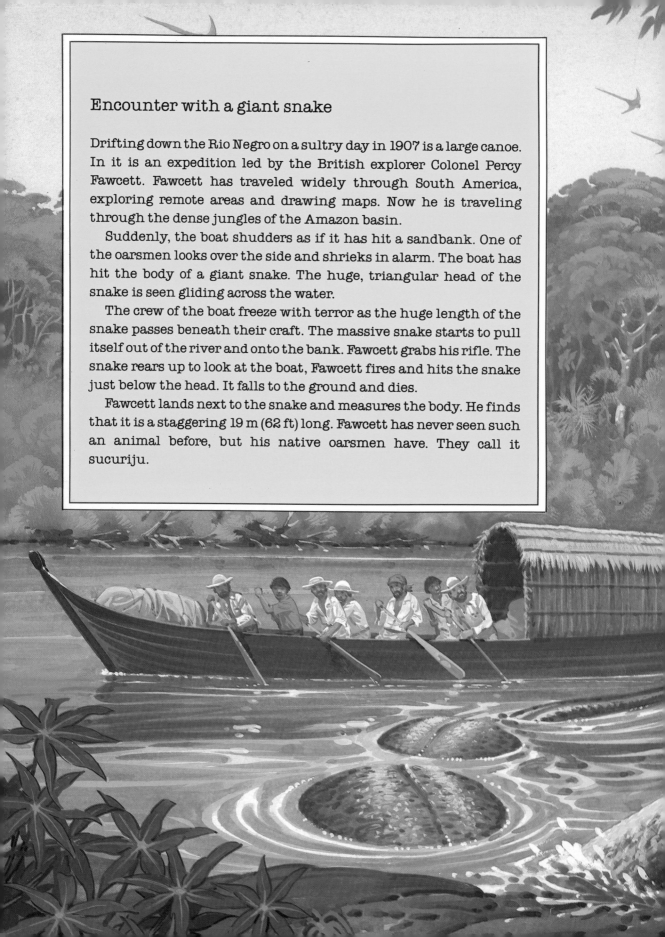

Encounter with a giant snake

Drifting down the Rio Negro on a sultry day in 1907 is a large canoe. In it is an expedition led by the British explorer Colonel Percy Fawcett. Fawcett has traveled widely through South America, exploring remote areas and drawing maps. Now he is traveling through the dense jungles of the Amazon basin.

Suddenly, the boat shudders as if it has hit a sandbank. One of the oarsmen looks over the side and shrieks in alarm. The boat has hit the body of a giant snake. The huge, triangular head of the snake is seen gliding across the water.

The crew of the boat freeze with terror as the huge length of the snake passes beneath their craft. The massive snake starts to pull itself out of the river and onto the bank. Fawcett grabs his rifle. The snake rears up to look at the boat, Fawcett fires and hits the snake just below the head. It falls to the ground and dies.

Fawcett lands next to the snake and measures the body. He finds that it is a staggering 19 m (62 ft) long. Fawcett has never seen such an animal before, but his native oarsmen have. They call it sucuriju.

The sucuriju

A winding tributary of the Amazon River. It is in the thick rain forests of the Amazon basin that the sucuriju is thought to live.

A rock python swallowing a Thomson's gazelle. Pythons are constricting snakes, which means that they kill their prey by squeezing it to death.

The Amazonian rain forest is a vast and unexplored territory. Though large areas of the forest are being felled each year, there is a huge amount of territory still blanketed by the trees. The Amazon River drains nearly two million square miles of land. Most of this is covered by rain forest. This forest, as its name suggests, receives large amounts of rain nearly every day. The whole woodland is warm and wet. It is an ideal environment in which plants and animals can thrive. This rain forest is indeed packed with thousands of species of plants and animals. Every year scientists discover new species in this prolific area. Most of these discoveries are of small forms of life, such as insects, frogs or tiny flowers. However, there are persistent reports of one very large type of animal that scientists have not yet found. This is known as the sucuriju.

This horrifying beast is said to be a giant snake well over 30 m (98 ft) long. The largest snake known to science is the reticulated python, one specimen of which measured 10 m (33 ft) in length. However, reports of larger snakes have been filtering out of the Amazon for many years. These snakes are said to be constricting snakes, and are often referred to as giant anacondas. The anaconda is a species of snake common in the Amazon. Constricting snakes kill their prey by squeezing, rather than by poison. The snake coils itself around the victim and squeezes its prey until it cannot breathe and dies of suffocation. The snake then swallows it whole. Large pythons are capable of eating sheep. So, if the sucuriju exists, it would be capable of eating any animal in the river basin.

Although many people have reported seeing, or even shooting the sucuriju, the snake is still not recognized by science. The experience of Colonel Percy Fawcett is fairly typical from this point of view. Fawcett was a well-known and highly respected explorer. If he said that he had traveled along a certain river and that it flowed in a certain direction, people believed him. When he shot a giant snake on the banks of the Rio Negro, he was hundreds of miles from civilization. It was impossible for him to carry the dead snake with him, so Fawcett had to leave it where it was. When Fawcett returned to Europe, he found that nobody believed his story about the sucuriju. He became the victim of public ridicule.

In 1948, a photograph was taken of a dead sucuriju that had been killed near the town of Manaos. The body was disposed of before scientists could examine it.

In 1948 a sucuriju was killed near the town of Manaos in Brazil by a man armed with a machine gun. Local officials measured the snake. They found it was 40 m (130 ft) long, a meter wide and weighed an estimated 5 tons. A photograph was taken of the sucuriju that appeared in the local newspaper. Unfortunately, the body of the snake was disposed of before any scientists heard about it.

Snake trails that are no less than 2 m (6½ ft) wide have been found in the jungle. The size of a snake able to leave such a trail is terrible to think about.

These reports, and others, seem enough evidence to indicate that a truly enormous type of snake really is prowling through the Amazonian rain forest. There is certainly enough food available in the forests to keep such an animal alive.

As with so many other unrecorded animals, science is waiting for a specimen to be caught and brought back for study. With the rain forests being felled at a great rate, it may not be long before a sucuriju is found and the species recognized in the world of science.

The Amazon rain forest is currently being felled at an alarming rate. Although this may increase our chances of discovering a live sucuriju, it will also destroy the habitat in which the creature lives.

Date chart

1907   Colonel Percy Fawcett shoots a 19-m (62-ft) sucuriju on the banks of the Rio Negro.

1933   Local tribesmen report killing a snake so large that four men could not lift its head from the ground.

1948   A 40-m (130-ft) sucuriju is killed near Manaos.

1954   A 38-m (125-ft) snake is killed by an army patrol in the rain forest near Amapa, Brazil.

1988   Continuing felling of the rain forest may lead to the discovery of a sucuriju.

Left Colonel Percy Fawcett in 1911.

Large constricting snakes are known to eat fairly large animals. If the sucuriju exists, it is clearly able to kill and eat any other animal in the rain forest, even humans. People who live in the rain forest have no doubt that the sucuriju exists and usually do their best to avoid the creature. Beside the Rio Jacare is a lonely tombstone dedicated to the memory of a Welshman named Thomas. He came to the region and was eaten by a mysterious beast that, from descriptions of native witnesses, sounds very like a sucuriju. Of all the mysterious monsters in this book, the sucuriju seems to be the most dangerous.

In this book we have considered information concerning several large animals which are said to exist, but which scientists have refused to accept as genuine. The only evidence for their existence is that of eyewitnesses and some photographs. Scientists, probably rightly, do not accept these as conclusive proof.

It is likely that in many cases people have been mistaken in what they saw. Perhaps reports have been exaggerated and people have added details in order to make their stories more exciting. It is even possible that some people have deliberately invented stories and faked photographs so that they could see their names in the newspapers. On the other hand, it seems most unlikely that every one of these witnesses has been mistaken or untruthful.

We usually think that every corner of our planet has been carefully explored, but this is far from the truth. Vast areas of land and sea remain almost entirely unfrequented by humans. With the exception of the Loch Ness monster, the animals featured in this book are said to live in these unexplored areas. It is entirely possible that these large

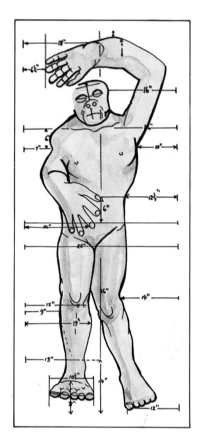

In 1968, this "ape-man" was discovered frozen in a block of ice in Minnesota. It was being used as an exhibit in a traveling show. Fearing investigation by the authorities, the owner disposed of the body and replaced it with a model. Was it a sasquatch?

Left *Earlier this century the existence of the okapi was not recognized by scientists. Only when they have a specimen to study will they accept that a previously unheard-of species actually exists.*

Gong Yulan (the woman standing by the tree) tells a group of soldiers how she saw a "wildman" on June 19, 1976, in Hubei Province, China.

animals do exist, but that is not the same as saying that they actually do. The evidence in favor of their existence is far from conclusive.

At the beginning of the century the okapi, the gorilla and the Mongolian wild horse were unrecognized by science. A few people reported seeing these creatures, but science refused to accept them as real animals. It was only when — at last — somebody brought back a live or dead specimen that the animals were accepted as genuine. Who knows, perhaps the scientists will one day be obliged to accept the existence of the creatures featured in this book?

45

Glossary

Anaconda   A large snake that crushes its prey.

Archaeological   Relating to the study of objects and remains from ancient times.

Basin (as in the Congo or Amazon basins) The area of countryside drained by a river and its tributaries.

Cascade   To tumble down, like a waterfall.

Conclusive   Decisive; final; putting an end to doubt.

Coniferous forest   A forest made up largely of conifers; that is, evergreen trees that bear cones (such as fir or pine trees).

Constricting snakes   Snakes that kill their prey by coiling their bodies around the animal and squeezing it until it suffocates.

Culture   The lifestyle or civilization of a race of people or a period in history.

Dinosaur   Any of the huge species of reptiles that lived more than 65 million years ago.

Evidence   A clear sign or indication.

Eyewitness   Someone who actually sees a thing happening.

Fossil   The remains, impression or trace of an animal or plant found preserved in rock.

Genuine   Real; not artificial or false.

Herbivores   Animals that feed only on plants.

Himalayas   The world's highest mountain range, which runs for 2,400 km (1,491 mi) across southern Asia. Mount Everest, the highest mountain in the world, is part of the Himalayas.

Hour-glass   An instrument for measuring hours by the running of sand from one glass, through a narrow opening, into another. It takes exactly one hour for the sand to run through.

Incident   A happening; an event.

Indistinct   Unclear.

Middle Ages   The period of history from about AD 1000 to 1500.

Neanderthal   Describing an early form of man, believed to have died out around 40,000 years ago.

Orangutan   A large, human-like ape, reddish-brown in color.

Above *Paul Freeman, who saw a sasquatch and its footprints in Umatilla National Forest.*

Rain forest   A dense forest of evergreen trees in an area of very heavy rainfall.

Reticulated python   The largest snake known to science, which moves forward in almost a straight line by using the scales underneath its body. It is also a constricting snake.

Sauropod   A type of four-footed, plant-eating dinosaur, with a small head and a long neck and tail.

Sherpa   A member of a Tibetan people living on the southern slopes of the Himalayas in Nepal, well known for their mountaineering skills.

Sonar   Equipment that can detect objects under the water or find out how deep a body of water is by sending out pulses of sound and measuring the echoes.

Suffocation   The act of choking a person or animal by keeping them from breathing.

Sultry   Very hot and humid.

Trapper   A person who traps animals, especially for their furs or skins.

Yak   A long-haired ox found in Tibet.

Further reading

The following books will tell you more about some of the monsters mentioned in this book:

The Abominable Snowcreature by Stephen Rudley. NY: Franklin Watts, 1978.

Bigfoot: Man, Monster or Myth? by Carrie Carmichael. Milwaukee, WI: Raintree Publishers, 1977.

The Bigfoot Mystery by Lynn Sonberg. NY: Bantam, 1983.

The Greatest Monsters in the World by Daniel Cohen. NY: Archway, 1977.

The Monster of Loch Ness by James Cornell. NY: Scholastic, Inc. 1978.

Monsters, Mysteries, UFOs by Linda Spellman. Santa Barbara, CA: The Learning Works, 1984.

Monsters: A Reference First Book by Rhoda Blumberg. NY: Franklin Watts, 1983.

__Below__ This monster is said to have terrorized the waters of Lake Utopia, Canada, for many years.

Index

Picture Acknowledgments

The publishers would like to thank the following for supplying pictures for use in this book: Bruce Coleman 40 (bottom), 44 (bottom); Mary Evans Picture Library 18; Fortean Picture Library 7 (top and bottom), 15 (top, Nicholas Witchell), 15 (bottom), 19 (bottom), 29 (left, René Dahinden), 30 (bottom, René Dahinden), 43, 45 (Dr. Zhou Gouxing), 46 (René Dahinden), 47; Geoscience Features 6; Mountain Camera John Cleare 23 (top), 25 (left and right); PHOTRI 14; Tony Morrison/South American Pictures 40 (top), 42; TOPHAM 11 (bottom), 22, 36. All artwork is by Bernard Long, except the following by Stephen Wheele: 11 (top), 12, 19, (top), 23 (bottom), 31, 36, 44 (top).